ATMOSPHERE IN DANGER

© Aladdin Books Ltd 2005

*New edition published in the
United States in 2005 by:*
Stargazer Books
c/o The Creative Company
123 South Broad Street
P.O. Box 227
Mankato, Minnesota 56002

Designer: Keith Newell
Editors: Sally Matthews
            Brian Hunter Smart
Picture Research: Emma Krikler
                Brian Hunter Smart
Illustrator: Mike Saunders
Consultant: Jacky Karas,
            Friends of the Earth

Printed in UAE

Library of Congress Cataloging-in-Publication Data

Walker, Jane (Jane Alison)
   Atmosphere in danger / by Jane Walker. --New ed.
      p. cm.-- (Environmental disasters)
   Includes index.
   ISBN 1-932799-12-5 (alk. paper)
      1. Air--Pollution--Juvenile literature.
      2. Air quality management--Juvenile literature. I. Title.

TD 883.13.W94 2004
363.739'2--dc22
                                                    2003070750

Environmental Disasters

ATMOSPHERE IN DANGER

JANE WALKER

STARGAZER BOOKS

CONTENTS

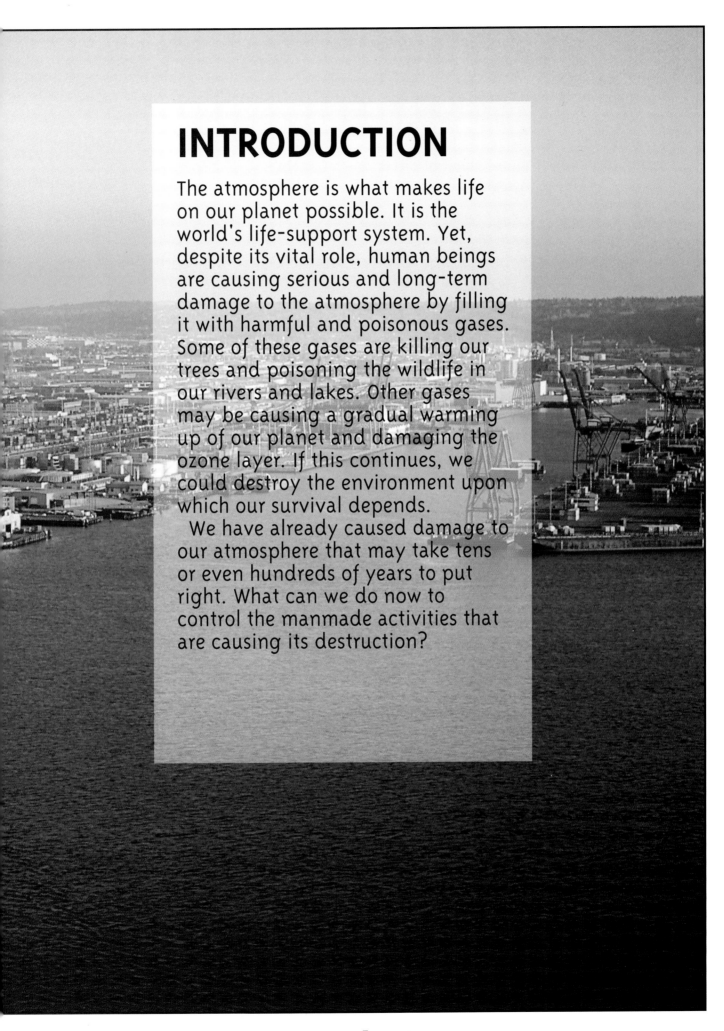

INTRODUCTION

The atmosphere is what makes life on our planet possible. It is the world's life-support system. Yet, despite its vital role, human beings are causing serious and long-term damage to the atmosphere by filling it with harmful and poisonous gases. Some of these gases are killing our trees and poisoning the wildlife in our rivers and lakes. Other gases may be causing a gradual warming up of our planet and damaging the ozone layer. If this continues, we could destroy the environment upon which our survival depends.

We have already caused damage to our atmosphere that may take tens or even hundreds of years to put right. What can we do now to control the manmade activities that are causing its destruction?

THE ATMOSPHERE

The earth is surrounded by layers of air that together make up the atmosphere. Air consists of a mixture of different gases that all living things need in order to stay alive. Human beings and other animals breathe in oxygen and breathe out carbon dioxide. Generally, trees and other plants take in carbon dioxide and release huge amounts of oxygen back into the air.

The atmosphere extends for over 250 miles (400 km) above the earth's surface. It can be divided into several different layers. The troposphere is the layer closest to the earth. This contains the air we breathe and the weather, including wind, clouds, rain, and snow. It reaches up for about 14.5 miles (23 km) over the equator, but is much thinner over the poles, where it extends for only about 3.7 miles (6 km).

The next layer is called the stratosphere. This stretches from around 9 to 30 miles (15-50 km) above the earth's surface. It is where jet airplanes fly and it contains the ozone layer, which protects us from the sun's harmful rays.

↓ The satellite picture (below) shows the clouds in the atmosphere surrounding the earth's surface. Through the clouds, you can see the Arabian peninsula and the east coast of Africa.

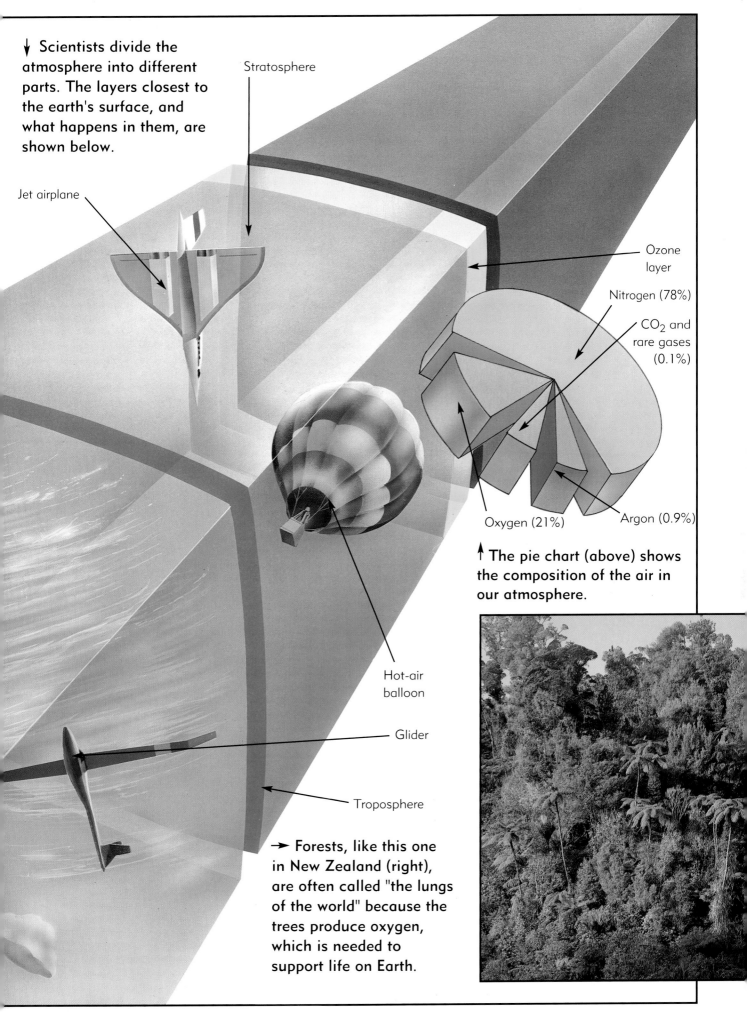

↓ Scientists divide the atmosphere into different parts. The layers closest to the earth's surface, and what happens in them, are shown below.

Stratosphere

Jet airplane

Ozone layer

Nitrogen (78%)

CO_2 and rare gases (0.1%)

Oxygen (21%)

Argon (0.9%)

↑ The pie chart (above) shows the composition of the air in our atmosphere.

Hot-air balloon

Glider

Troposphere

→ Forests, like this one in New Zealand (right), are often called "the lungs of the world" because the trees produce oxygen, which is needed to support life on Earth.

7

POLLUTING THE AIR

Human beings are making the air dirtier and dirtier. As the demand for energy has increased, more and more harmful gases have been produced as a result of burning fossil fuels, such as coal, oil, and gas. Two of the principal air pollutants are sulfur dioxide (SO_2) and nitrogen oxide (NO_2), which are the main causes of acid rain (see page 16).

We are also increasing the quantity of gases that trap heat in the atmosphere. These include carbon dioxide (CO_2), which is released by the burning of fossil fuels and rainforest destruction, and methane, which is released from rice fields, swamps, and animal waste.

Another type of air pollution comes from manmade chemicals such as chlorofluorocarbons (CFCs). These rise into the atmosphere and damage the ozone layer.

↓ Around 50% of the world's tropical rainforests have been destroyed. When they are burned, like the one in Colombia (below), they release large quantities of carbon dioxide into the atmosphere.

Burning trees release carbon dioxide.

Deforestation

With fewer trees, less carbon dioxide is absorbed from the atmosphere.

↓ Power plants, industry, and cars are the principal sources of sulfur dioxide and carbon dioxide. They account for around two-thirds of global CO_2 emissions and over half of all SO_2 emissions.

Power plants burn fossil fuels.

↑ Los Angeles (above) suffers from serious air pollution caused by car exhaust fumes. These contain SO_2, CO_2, and other poisonous gases.

↓ Copsa Mica, in Romania (below), is one of the world's most polluted cities. Its air is filled with harmful gases produced by industry.

City smog

Exhaust gases from automobiles

Grazing cattle release methane.

WARMING THE EARTH

The earth is kept warm by heat from the sun, which is trapped in the atmosphere by gases acting rather like the glass in a greenhouse. These gases allow some of the sun's warming rays to come in, and prevent some of the heat from escaping back into space. This makes life on our planet possible and is known as the "greenhouse effect."

In recent years, the volume of greenhouse gases in the atmosphere has steadily increased. Scientists are concerned that these gases may be causing the world to heat up. They call this effect "global warming."

Carbon dioxide is the main greenhouse gas. However, there are other gases that are present in the atmosphere in smaller quantities, but are far more effective at trapping the sun's heat. They include CFCs, methane, nitrous oxide, and ground-level ozone (which is different from that found in the ozone layer—see page 14).

→ The sun's rays pass through the atmosphere to reach the earth. As the rays try to escape back into space, they are either absorbed by the greenhouse gases or reflected back onto the earth's surface.

↓ Methane is a greenhouse gas given off by decaying human and animal waste, swamps, and other waterlogged areas, such as this rice field in Bali (below).

Trapped heat

10

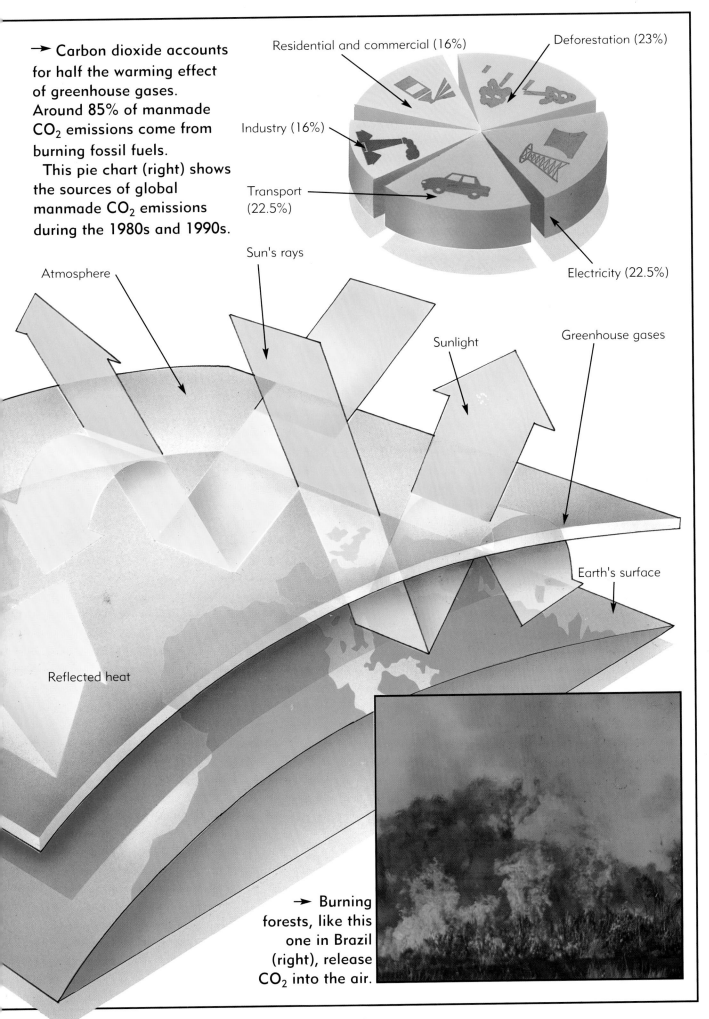

→ Carbon dioxide accounts for half the warming effect of greenhouse gases. Around 85% of manmade CO_2 emissions come from burning fossil fuels.

This pie chart (right) shows the sources of global manmade CO_2 emissions during the 1980s and 1990s.

Residential and commercial (16%)

Deforestation (23%)

Industry (16%)

Transport (22.5%)

Electricity (22.5%)

Sun's rays

Atmosphere

Sunlight

Greenhouse gases

Earth's surface

Reflected heat

→ Burning forests, like this one in Brazil (right), release CO_2 into the air.

A CHANGING WORLD

Scientists believe that global warming may be responsible for important changes in the world's climate and the environment.

Altered patterns of rainfall could result in periods of drought in some areas that do not traditionally suffer from water shortages, such as the Great Plains in the United States—a major cereal-growing area. Other parts of the world may experience more rainfall, for example certain monsoon areas in southern Asia. There could also be an increase in the number of extreme weather events, such as hurricanes, floods, and droughts.

As the world's climate changes, many plant and animal species could face extinction as their natural habitats change or disappear.

Temperature increases could also lead to a rise in world sea levels. This could cause serious flooding in some areas, threatening the homes and livelihoods of more than 30% of the world's population.

↓ Temperature rises may lead to more droughts. This could cause the land to become parched and unproductive, and many rivers and lakes, like this one in Kenya (below), to dry up. As a result, there could be large-scale crop failures, grain shortages, and famine.

↓ In a warmer world, sea levels will probably rise. Many low-lying, densely populated cities by the sea, like St. Petersburg in Russia, New Orleans in the U.S., and Venice in Italy (below) could be left uninhabitable by a 6 ft rise in sea levels.

↑ In the 1990s, there were severe hurricanes throughout Europe that caused enormous damage (above). Hurricanes are almost unknown in this area. However, in a hotter world, storms like this could become more frequent.

↓ With a sea level rise of around 3 feet, some very low-lying islands, such as this one off Papua New Guinea in the Pacific Ocean (below), could completely disappear.

THE OZONE LAYER

The ozone layer is a band of gas that prevents the sun's harmful ultraviolet rays from reaching the earth. We have been damaging this protective barrier by destroying the ozone inside it.

When chemicals, such as halons, methyl bromide, and chlorofluorocarbons (CFCs) rise into the atmosphere, they release chloride and bromine. These gases attack and destroy ozone.

Until recently, CFCs were used in air-conditioning units, refrigerators, and freezers, and in the manufacture of foam products. Halons were used in fire extinguishers and methyl bromide was used to fumigate soil and food-storage areas.

CFCs can remain in the atmosphere for more than 100 years, continuing to attack the ozone layer.

⋏ As the ozone layer gets thinner, more of the sun's ultraviolet (UV) rays reach the earth's surface. People who spend a lot of time in the sun, like the sunbathers above, are at risk from the damaging effects of too much UV radiation. It can cause skin cancers and eye problems, and is particularly harmful to fair-skinned people.

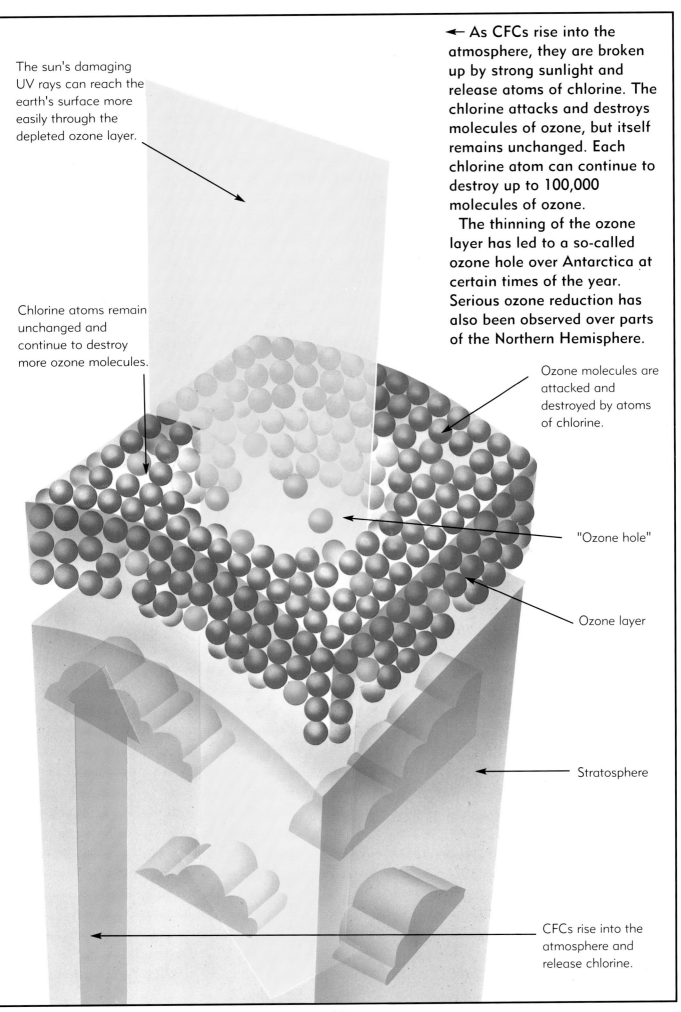

The sun's damaging UV rays can reach the earth's surface more easily through the depleted ozone layer.

← As CFCs rise into the atmosphere, they are broken up by strong sunlight and release atoms of chlorine. The chlorine attacks and destroys molecules of ozone, but itself remains unchanged. Each chlorine atom can continue to destroy up to 100,000 molecules of ozone.

The thinning of the ozone layer has led to a so-called ozone hole over Antarctica at certain times of the year. Serious ozone reduction has also been observed over parts of the Northern Hemisphere.

Chlorine atoms remain unchanged and continue to destroy more ozone molecules.

Ozone molecules are attacked and destroyed by atoms of chlorine.

"Ozone hole"

Ozone layer

Stratosphere

CFCs rise into the atmosphere and release chlorine.

WHAT IS ACID RAIN?

Acid rain is formed when air pollutants mix with water in the atmosphere to form weak acids. These fall down to the earth as acid rain, hail, snow, mist, or fog.

The main causes of acid rain are sulfur dioxide and nitrogen oxides, released in large quantities when fossil fuels are burned in factories, power plants, and car engines.

Eastern European countries, such as Poland and Slovakia, have very serious problems with acid rain. This is because the type of coal they burn releases large quantities of sulfur dioxide.

Acid rain often falls a long distance from where it is produced. The United States gives off gases that fall as acid rain in Canada.

↑ Tall factory chimneys, like those above, lift pollution high into the air. Here, it can be carried for long distances in the clouds, before falling as acid rain far away from its original source.

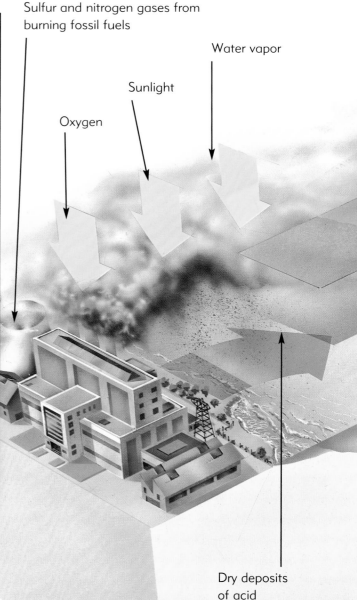

Sulfur and nitrogen gases from burning fossil fuels

Water vapor

Sunlight

Oxygen

Dry deposits of acid

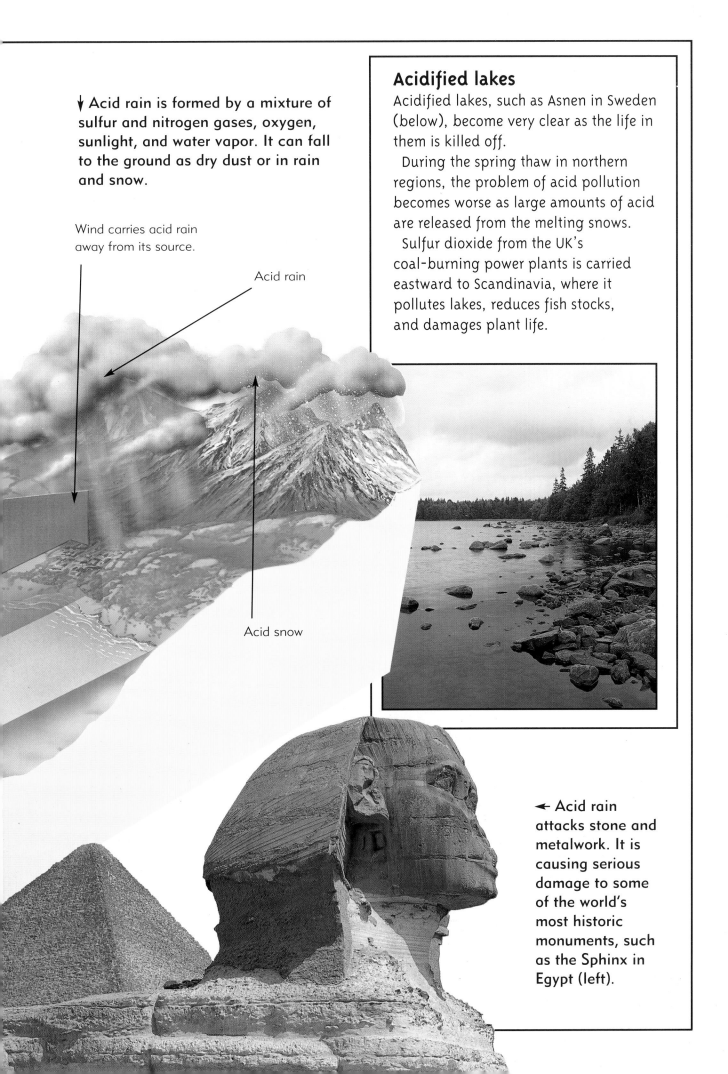

↓ Acid rain is formed by a mixture of sulfur and nitrogen gases, oxygen, sunlight, and water vapor. It can fall to the ground as dry dust or in rain and snow.

Wind carries acid rain away from its source.

Acid rain

Acid snow

Acidified lakes

Acidified lakes, such as Asnen in Sweden (below), become very clear as the life in them is killed off.

During the spring thaw in northern regions, the problem of acid pollution becomes worse as large amounts of acid are released from the melting snows.

Sulfur dioxide from the UK's coal-burning power plants is carried eastward to Scandinavia, where it pollutes lakes, reduces fish stocks, and damages plant life.

← Acid rain attacks stone and metalwork. It is causing serious damage to some of the world's most historic monuments, such as the Sphinx in Egypt (left).

DEATH ACROSS THE WORLD

Acid rain is damaging the soil, poisoning the lakes and rivers, and devastating the forests of Europe and North America. Over 60 percent of coniferous trees in the United Kingdom, and more than half of all trees in Germany, have been affected by acid rain. It is also responsible for serious damage to sugar maple trees in Canada.

Acid rain attacks trees through both the air and soil, resulting in the discoloration and loss of leaves. The weakened trees are then more likely to be harmed by insects and disease.

Acid rain also damages rivers, lakes, and streams by making their water too acidic. This destroys many forms of life, including water plants, insects, fish, and fish-eating creatures.

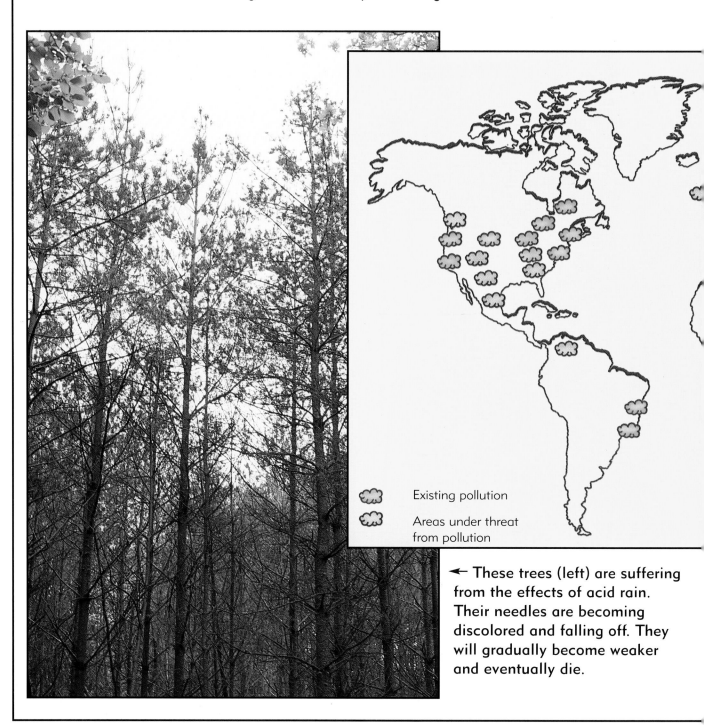

Existing pollution

Areas under threat from pollution

← These trees (left) are suffering from the effects of acid rain. Their needles are becoming discolored and falling off. They will gradually become weaker and eventually die.

↑ This lake in Wales, in the UK, (above) shows the sinister beauty of an acidified landscape. There is no life in its clear blue water and the acid-infected trees are dying.

↓ Fish cannot survive in highly acidified water. They die from poisoning or loss of their food supply. The fish population of many lakes and rivers affected by acid rain is slowly disappearing.

↑ Acid rain is a worldwide problem. However, most of the air pollution that causes it is produced in industrial areas. The distribution of acid rain pollution is shown in the diagram above.

POISONS IN THE AIR

The air in many cities and towns is filled with harmful and often poisonous substances. One of the most dangerous of these is lead, much of which enters the air from vehicle exhausts. Leaded gasoline was introduced when scientists discovered that it made cars run more efficiently. But the poisonous fumes from lead can cause many nervous and mental disorders, and are particularly dangerous to children.

In the 20th century, many large industrial cities were affected by "smog," a combination of smoke and poisonous gases. Today, they suffer from a more dangerous type of smog called photochemical smog. This contains a poisonous combination of substances, including hydrocarbons, nitrogen oxides, carbon monoxide, and ground-level ozone. It irritates people's eyes and lungs and makes breathing difficult. It can also cause respiratory illnesses and cancer.

↓ The exhaust fumes from cars are full of poisonous gases. These include hydrocarbons and carbon monoxide, that form photochemical smog.

↓ Large quantities of poisons are released into the air by cars, factories, and power plants. Some of the worst air pollution occurs in the industrial cities of the developing world, where pollution controls are not so strict.

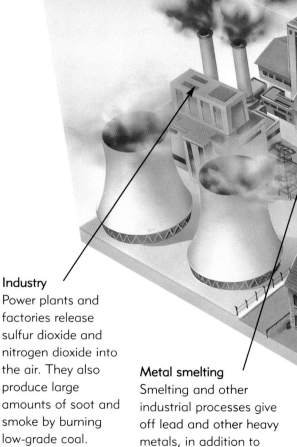

Industry
Power plants and factories release sulfur dioxide and nitrogen dioxide into the air. They also produce large amounts of soot and smoke by burning low-grade coal.

Metal smelting
Smelting and other industrial processes give off lead and other heavy metals, in addition to smoke and soot.

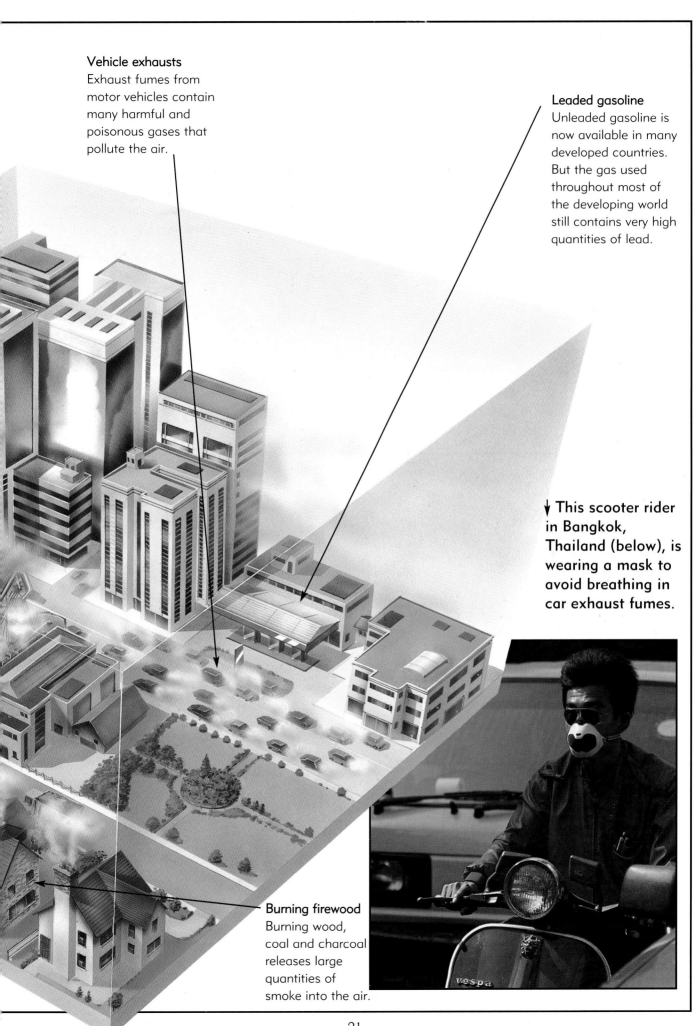

Vehicle exhausts
Exhaust fumes from motor vehicles contain many harmful and poisonous gases that pollute the air.

Leaded gasoline
Unleaded gasoline is now available in many developed countries. But the gas used throughout most of the developing world still contains very high quantities of lead.

↓ This scooter rider in Bangkok, Thailand (below), is wearing a mask to avoid breathing in car exhaust fumes.

Burning firewood
Burning wood, coal and charcoal releases large quantities of smoke into the air.

DISASTERS IN HISTORY

In 1984, more than 5,000 people died when poisonous gas escaped from a pesticide factory in the Indian city of Bhopal. Some of the survivors were blinded instantly, or later suffered serious eye injuries. Others experienced breathing and digestive problems.

Less than 18 months later, following an accident at the Chernobyl nuclear power plant in the former Soviet Union, a deadly, radioactive cloud was blown across Europe. Only a few deaths were reported immediately after the accident. However, the long-term damage to the health of local people and workers at the plant is far more serious. People exposed to high doses of radioactivity run a strong risk of developing leukemia and other forms of cancer. Farther away, the radioactivity contaminated large numbers of reindeer in Finland and hill-grazing sheep in Scotland.

Chernobyl

Radioactive cloud

↑ After an explosion in a reactor at the Chernobyl nuclear plant, a vast radioactive cloud spread over an area measuring 1,800 miles across, covering much of Europe (above).

← These Soviet workers (left) are measuring the radiation levels in the crop fields around the Chernobyl plant.

Cubatão, Brazil

Another kind of manmade disaster has occurred in the Brazilian town of Cubatão, near São Paulo (below), an area referred to as the "Valley of Death."

The lack of environmental regulations and controls and an abundance of cheap labor in Brazil, has attracted many foreign companies to towns such as Cubatão. These companies have been developing industry there since the 1950s. They now own more than 50% of the area's factories.

The levels of industrial pollution in Cubatão would be unacceptable in the developed world. Over a number of decades this pollution has caused long-term damage to the local people and their environment. Respiratory disease and malformed babies are common, and about 30% of deaths in the area are caused by pollution-related illnesses.

⬆ An explosion at a herbicide factory in Seveso, Italy (above), in **1976**, released a cloud of poisonous gas. Thousands of people suffered from poisoning and large areas of land were contaminated.

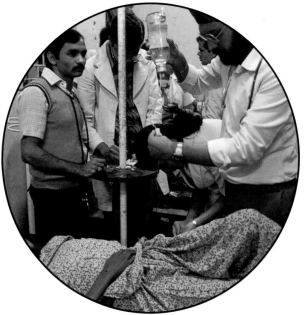

⬆ Doctors treat a victim of the Bhopal disaster (above). The poisonous gas from the Union Carbide factory affected about **30,000 to 40,000** people living nearby.

REPAIRING THE DAMAGE

There are a number of measures that we can take to repair some of the damage we have inflicted on the earth's atmosphere and our environment.

Acid-affected lakes and forests can be treated with powdered lime. Once the acidity has been removed, fish can return to the treated waters and young trees will grow healthily in the soil. But treatment with lime can do nothing to reverse the process of destruction or control the source of the acid pollution.

Reforestation programs involving the large-scale planting of trees, would increase the carbon "sink," a term used to describe the way in which trees remove the carbon dioxide from the air. However, to absorb the total output of manmade CO_2 in the world today, an area of tropical forest the size of Europe, from the Atlantic to the Urals would have to be planted.

There has been some success in the fight to protect the ozone layer, with the development of "ozone-friendly" products, manufactured without using CFCs. In 1992, the phase-out date for CFCs was brought forward to 1995. Developing countries were given a further ten years from this date, and a fund was established to assist the development of CFC-free chemicals.

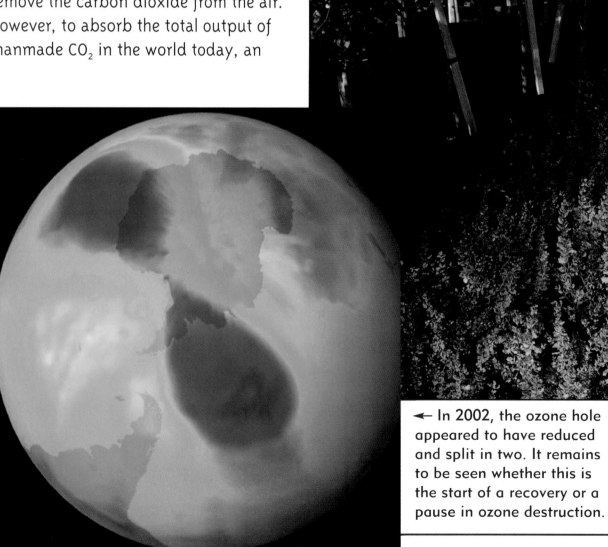

← In 2002, the ozone hole appeared to have reduced and split in two. It remains to be seen whether this is the start of a recovery or a pause in ozone destruction.

→ Helicopters are used to pour tons of powdered lime over lakes to neutralize their acidity (right). This is short-term, difficult, and expensive and only controls the symptoms rather than the causes of acid pollution.

↓ Tree-planting schemes, like this one in the U.S. (below), replace trees that have been lost due to acid pollution, deforestation, and storm damage.

→ Air management schemes introduced into cities, like Los Angeles, aim to improve the air quality. This glass suction tube (right) takes in air for analysis.

↓ Controls on the exhaust emissions of motor vehicles are vital in the fight against photochemical smog. Smog check stations, like the one below, have been introduced to test and control the output of exhaust gases.

↓ Giant, and very expensive, cleaning devices called "scrubbers" can be fitted to the chimneys of power plants, like this one at the Akou power plant in Japan (below). As waste gases pass through the scrubbers, they are sprayed with a mixture of limestone and water. This reacts with the sulfur dioxide, removing most of it from the waste gases before they are released into the atmosphere. Scrubbers can reduce SO_2 emissions by up to 90 percent.

← Recycling schemes, such as this paper recycling plant (left), can save energy and reduce air pollution. They slow down the use of limited natural resources and cut down on waste. Paper, glass, metal, plastic, and even oil can be recycled.

A CLEANER ATMOSPHERE

The industrialized world is now taking action to clean up our air.

The United States and the European Community have been working to reduce their output of sulfur dioxide and nitrogen oxides by setting strict targets for reduction. With the continued replacement of coal-fired power plants and the increased use of desulfurization equipment, emissions are expected to decline. Yet, far greater reductions are needed to improve our environment.

Many countries have introduced strict regulations on car exhaust emissions. In the state of California, these include car pooling, a complete ban on leaded gasoline, and the fitting of catalytic converters on all cars. At the beginning of this century, 5% of all new vehicles in California were required to have no harmful exhaust emissions.

To control carbon dioxide levels in the atmosphere, we must take further measures to reduce our use of fossil fuels and stop the destruction of tropical rainforests.

Pollution control can be very expensive. As progress is made by the developed world, it is important to ensure that poorer countries can also afford to develop nonpolluting forms of industrial processing and energy production.

➤ Electric cars like the "Twin" (right) are part of a big push to develop cleaner cars. More efficient engines using different fuels are being designed.

THE FUTURE

The introduction of a tax on polluting forms of energy may help reduce our use of fossil fuels. It would encourage people and industry to save energy and develop less polluting forms of energy, including solar, wind, and water power.

Garbage and waste materials from humans and animals can be used to provide energy and organic fertilizers. Pioneering schemes at garbage dumps in North America and Europe, convert methane, a greenhouse gas, into electricity. Organic fertilizers can be used instead of artificial fertilizers, which release nitrous oxide, a cause of acid rain.

Solar glazing uses the sun's rays to heat up buildings, such as these offices in Liverpool, England (below).

With more than 500 million cars in use in the world today, we need to design vehicles that run on cleaner forms of energy, such as battery packs and fuel cells. Fuel cells release no harmful gases and can be used to power anything from electric cars to factories.

Solar power
Solar panels convert the sun's energy into electricity.

Wind power
The turning blades of wind turbines drive generators, which make electricity.

Organic fertilizers
Farmers who change to organic fertilizers will help reduce the pollution caused by nitrous oxide, which is released by artificial fertilizers.

Cleaner cars
Unleaded gasoline, catalytic converters, battery packs, and fuel cells all reduce the harmful emissions from cars.

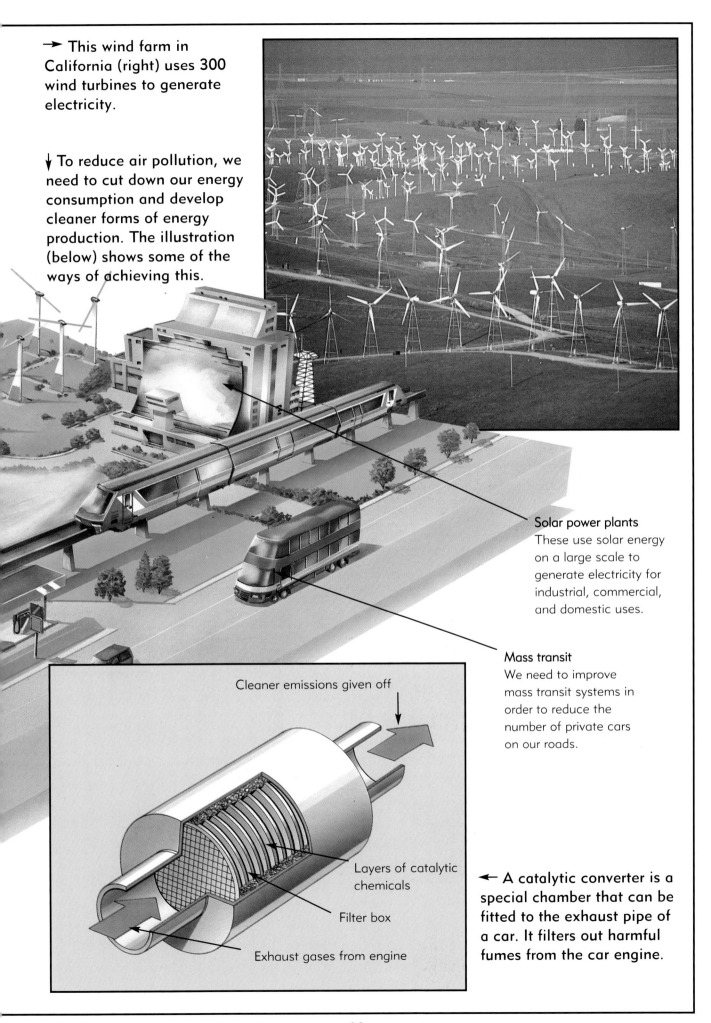

→ This wind farm in California (right) uses **300** wind turbines to generate electricity.

↓ To reduce air pollution, we need to cut down our energy consumption and develop cleaner forms of energy production. The illustration (below) shows some of the ways of achieving this.

Solar power plants
These use solar energy on a large scale to generate electricity for industrial, commercial, and domestic uses.

Mass transit
We need to improve mass transit systems in order to reduce the number of private cars on our roads.

Cleaner emissions given off

Layers of catalytic chemicals

Filter box

Exhaust gases from engine

← A catalytic converter is a special chamber that can be fitted to the exhaust pipe of a car. It filters out harmful fumes from the car engine.

FACT FILE

Acid rain

Acid rain causes serious corrosion to both soft building stones and metal. In the early 1980s, the copper plates of the Statue of Liberty were corroded by acid rain to such an extent that significant restoration was undertaken. Experts say that acid pollution has caused more damage to the Parthenon, in Greece, in the last 20 years than it sustained from natural forces in the previous 2,000 years.

London smog

In the smoke-filled city of London, smog levels reached alarming heights in the winter of 1952, when more than 4,000 people died as a result of smog-related illness.

Poisoning the Arctic

There is growing concern about the levels of highly poisonous chemicals found in people and animals living in the Arctic. The chemicals, used as pesticides, are called organochlorines. Some, including DDT, have been banned in the developed world.

The chemicals eventually evaporate into the air, particularly when used in warm climates. They are then carried in air currents through the atmosphere. When this chemical-laden air reaches the cold Arctic region, it cools and condenses, and the harmful chemicals fall onto the ice and snow. Once inside the bodies of animals, such as polar bears and seals, these chemicals can cause serious internal damage.

The ozone story

1972—annual world production of CFCs exceeds 750,000 tons.
1985—UK scientists discover an ozone hole over Antarctica.
1987—Antarctic ozone hole reaches the size of the United States. The Montreal Protocol sets legally binding controls on the production and consumption of ozone-depleting substances.
1992—deepest ozone hole ever recorded occurs over Antarctica and the tip of South America.
1993—ozone levels drop by between 12 and 14 percent over Europe and North America.
2002—ozone hole appears to have stabilized in Antarctica and may be reducing in size.
2050—If the phase-out imposed by the Montreal Protocol continues, recovery of the ozone layer is expected mid-century.

Global warming

Even if the world stops all greenhouse gas emissions immediately, it is predicted that global temperatures will rise another 3–9°F. Continuing temperature rises would lead to severe drought and shortfalls in food production. Famine might occur in areas not traditionally affected by food shortages.

Rising sea levels

Sea levels around the world have already risen by between 4 and 6 inches during the last century. Scientists estimate that sea levels may rise by a further 6–11 inches by the year 2050. This would put many of the world's largest cities, including London, Rio de Janeiro, Jakarta, and Hong Kong under threat.

In low-lying, densely populated countries, such as Bangladesh and Indonesia, the human cost of rising sea levels could be enormous. A rise of just 3 feet would leave millions of people in Bangladesh homeless and without land.

Disappearing rainforest

If we continue to destroy trees at the present rate we will soon run out. Today, less than 6% of the earth's surface is covered by rainforests. This compares to a figure of 15% in 1950. They also contain over half of the world's plant and animal species.

Recycling

The average American household produces roughly a ton of garbage per year, including bottles, cans, paper, and organic waste. About 80% of this could be recycled, yet little is. Recycling bottles, metals, and paper can slow down the use of limited natural resources, reduce the amount of garbage, and save energy. Every ton of glass recycled saves around 130 quarts of oil, and resmelting aluminum cans makes energy savings of 95%. Organic waste can be turned into compost and used instead of artificial fertilizers.

GLOSSARY

acid rain—rain that is made acidic when certain air pollutants react with water in the atmosphere. It can fall to the earth as rain, snow, mist, or dry particles of dust.

atmosphere—the different layers of gases that surround the earth.

carbon dioxide—the principal greenhouse gas in the atmosphere. It is released in large quantities when fossil fuels and rainforests are burned.

catalytic converter—a device that is fitted to a car to reduce the release of harmful gases, such as carbon monoxide, hydrocarbons, and nitrogen oxides.

chlorofluorocarbons (CFCs)—a group of manmade chemicals that release chlorine, which damages the ozone layer.

deforestation—the widespread destruction of forests by cutting down or burning trees.

emission—the release of gas or other substance.

extinction—the complete disappearance of a type of plant or animal from all areas of the world.

fossil fuel—a fuel that has been formed over millions of years from the remains of plants and animals buried in the ground. Coal, oil, and gas are fossil fuels.

global warming—a gradual rise in world temperatures caused by more heat being trapped in the atmosphere by greenhouse gases.

greenhouse effect—the sun's heat trapped by gases in the atmosphere, keeping the earth warm.

greenhouse gas—one of the gases in the atmosphere that keeps the earth warm by trapping heat from the sun.

methane—a greenhouse gas that is given off by decaying animal and plant waste, swamps, and other waterlogged areas.

nitrogen oxide—a gas that causes acid rain. The main sources are fossil fuel-burning power plants and automobiles.

ozone—a form of oxygen that is found in the lower and upper atmosphere. At ground level it is a highly poisonous part of photochemical smog.

ozone layer—a band of ozone gas in the upper atmosphere. It protects the earth from some of the sun's harmful rays.

photochemical smog—a kind of air pollution that forms a brownish haze over cities. It is formed when sunlight reacts with a variety of pollutants from cars and industry.

pollutant—a waste material that harms people or the environment.

recycling—reclaiming the useful materials from waste so that they can be used again.

reforestation—the replanting of trees in an area where the forest has been destroyed.

solar power—energy that is produced from the sun's rays.

stratosphere—the second lowest layer of the atmosphere, which contains the protective ozone layer.

sulfur dioxide—a gas that is given off when fossil fuels are burned. It helps form acid rain and photochemical smog.

troposphere—the lowest layer of the earth's atmosphere.

ultraviolet (UV) radiation—invisible rays from the sun. Too much UV radiation can cause skin cancer.

INDEX

Photocredits

Abbreviations: l-left, r-right, b-bottom, t-top, c-center, m-middle
Front cover l, back cover, 4-5, 9tr, 12-13 — Digital Stock. Front cover r, 3 — Corbis. 6, 29tr — Science Photo Library. 7, 22, 23 all, 25b — Frank Spooner Pictures. 8 — Bruce Coleman. 9b, 11, 12, 12-13, 14 — The Hutchinson Library. 10, 26t, 28bl — Eye Ubiquitous. 13t, 18, 19b — Charles de Vere. 13b — PhotoEssentials. 17b — Spectrum Colour Library. 17t — Environmental Picture Library. 19t, 20, 26b — Roger Vlitos. 21 — Panos Pictures. 24bl — NASA. 24-25 — U.S. Fish & Wildlife Service. 25t — Christen Agen, Swedish Environmental Research Institute. 26-27 — Courtesy of Babcock Hitachi. 27br — General Motors.